ISBN 978-1-84135-875-8

Copyright © 2012 Award Publications Limited

Illustrated by Jane Launchbury
Additional illustrations by Angela Hicks

All rights reserved. No part of this publication may be reproduced or utilized in any form or by any means electronic or mechanical, including photocopying, recording, or by any information storage and retrieval system now known or hereafter invented, without the prior written permission of the publisher.

First published as *Teddy's First Book of Prayers*
This edition first published 2012

Published by Award Publications Limited,
The Old Riding School, The Welbeck Estate,
Worksop, Nottinghamshire, S80 3LR

www.awardpublications.co.uk

Printed in Malaysia

My First Book of PRAYERS

Illustrated by Jane Launchbury

AWARD PUBLICATIONS LIMITED

The Lord's Prayer

Our Father, who art in heaven,
Hallowed be thy name,
Thy kingdom come,
Thy will be done on earth
As it is in heaven.
Give us this day our daily bread
And forgive us our trespasses
As we forgive them
That trespass against us.
And lead us not into temptation,
But deliver us from evil,
For thine is the kingdom,
The power and the glory,
For ever and ever.

Amen.

If you have plenty, be not greedy,
But share it with the poor and needy:
If you have a little, take good care,
To give the little birds a share.

As I lay me down to sleep,
I pray thee, God, my soul to keep;
And in the morning, when I wake
Please make me good for Jesus' sake.

Thank you for the world so sweet,
Thank you for the things we eat,
Thank you for the birds that sing,
Thank you, God, for everything.

Jesus bids us shine
With a pure, clear light;
Like a little candle
Burning in the night.

In this world of darkness
We must shine;
You in your small corner
And I in mine.

Praise God from whom all blessings flow;
Praise him, all creatures here below;
Praise him above, ye heavenly host;
Praise Father, Son and Holy Ghost.

Now the day is over,
Night is drawing nigh,
Shadows of the evening
Steal across the sky.

Now the darkness gathers,
Stars begin to peep,
Birds and beasts and flowers
Soon will be asleep.

Jesus give the weary
Calm and sweet repose;
With thy tenderest blessing
May our eyelids close.

Grant to little children
Visions bright of thee;
Guard the sailors tossing
On the deep blue sea.

When the morning wakens,
Then may I arise,
Pure, and fresh, and sinless
In thy holy eyes.

Thank you, God, for this new day
In my school to work and play.
Please be with me all day long,
In every story, game and song.
May all the happy things we do
Make you, our Father, happy too.

Lord, teach me all that I should know;
In grace and wisdom may I grow;
The more I learn to do thy will,
The better I may love thee still.

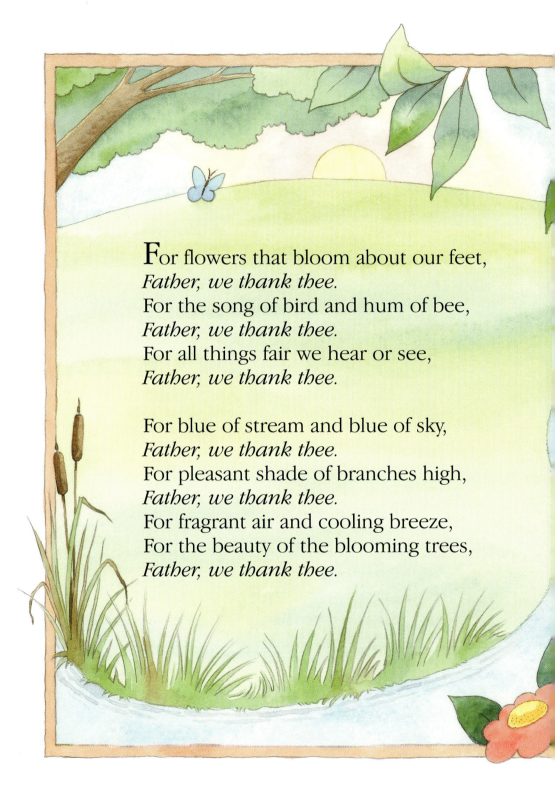

For flowers that bloom about our feet,
Father, we thank thee.
For the song of bird and hum of bee,
Father, we thank thee.
For all things fair we hear or see,
Father, we thank thee.

For blue of stream and blue of sky,
Father, we thank thee.
For pleasant shade of branches high,
Father, we thank thee.
For fragrant air and cooling breeze,
For the beauty of the blooming trees,
Father, we thank thee.

For this new morning with its light,
Father, we thank thee.
For the rest and shelter of the night,
Father, we thank thee.
For health and food, for love and friends,
For everything thy goodness sends,
Father, we thank thee.

Lord, make me an instrument of thy peace;
Where there is hatred, let me sow love;
Where there is injury, pardon;
Where there is discord, union;
Where there is doubt, faith;
Where there is despair, hope;
Where there is darkness, light;
Where there is sadness, joy.

Jesus, gentle shepherd, hear me,
Bless thy little lamb tonight.
Through the darkness be thou near me,
Watch my sleep till morning light.

All this day thy hand hath led me,
And I thank thee for thy care;
Thou hast clothed me, warmed and fed me;
Listen to my evening prayer.

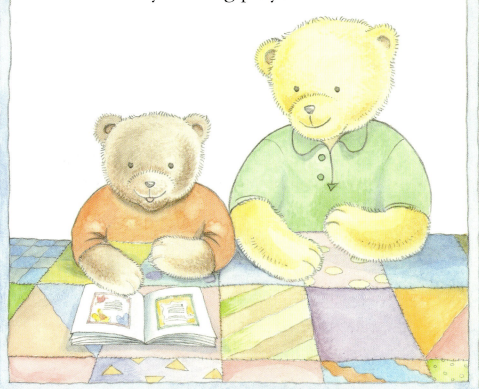

May we in safety sleep tonight,
From every danger free;
Because the darkness and the light
Are both alike to thee.

And when the rising sun displays
His cheerful beams abroad,
Then shall our grateful voice of praise
Declare thy goodness, Lord.

What can I give him,
Poor as I am?
if I were a shepherd
I would bring him a lamb;
If I were a wise man
I would do my part;
Yet what I can I give him –
Give my heart.

Thank you, Jesus, for this day,
For friends and family, work and play.
Now the night is here once more
I pray to you, my Saviour:
Take care of me while I sleep,
Place angels at my head and feet,
To see me through the dark of night,
And give me dreams full of cheer,
So when I wake in morning's light,
I'll wake rested, happy, with you near.

Thank you, Lord, for giving us this food today,
For those homeless and hungry let us pray,
That they may receive your blessing and care,
God bless your children, everywhere.

Father, lead me day by day,
Ever in thine own sweet way;
Teach me to be pure and true,
Show me what I ought to do.

When I'm tempted to do wrong,
Make me steadfast, wise and strong;
And when all alone I stand,
Shield me with thy mighty hand.

When my heart is full of glee,
Help me to remember thee;
Happy most of all to know
That my Father loves me so.

Bless these thy gifts, most gracious God
From whom all goodness springs,
Make clean our hearts and feed our souls
With good and joyful things.

Day by day, dear Lord of thee
Three things I pray:
To see thee more clearly,
To love thee more dearly,
To follow thee more nearly,
Day by day.

Your love, O Lord, reaches to the skies,
Above the clouds and into the heavens.
Your goodness is as mighty as the great
   mountains of the earth,
Your wisdom as deep as the ocean.

Count the ways I love you, O Lord,
By counting the stars in the sky.
My faith in you, is as sure as ocean tides.
I cannot be torn from you, O Lord,
Just as the sun cannot be torn from the sky.

I follow your teachings, O Lord,
As the river follows its path,
I spread your love and caring through the world
Like the flowers of your creation cast their seed.

With your love in my heart, O Lord,
Each glorious day you give to me,
I grow strong like the trees in the forests of
 your making,
And welcome others to share in your glory.

Good night! Good night!
Far flies the light;
But still God's love
Shall flame above,
Making all bright.
Good night! Good night!

Acknowledgements

Many of the prayers in this book are traditional
or by anonymous writers. Where authors are
known they are credited below:

page 11, Bishop Ken; page 12, S. Baring-Gould;
page 15, Isaac Watts; pages 16 & 17, Ralph Waldo Emerson;
page 18, St Francis of Assisi; page 19, Mary L. Duncan;
page 20, Jane Taylor; page 21, Christina Rossetti;
page 24, John Page Hopps; page 25 (bottom), St Richard of Chichester;
page 28, Victor Hugo